MW00616273

No ORDINARY Women

No Ordinary Women

Making a Difference through Righteous Influence

ELAINE S. DALTON

Salt Lake City, Utah

Photos on pages 4 and 11 provided by the author. Photo on page 11 by Busath Photography. Background image: New Line/shutterstock.com

Visit us at DeseretBook.com

Library of Congress Cataloging-in-Publication Data

Names: Dalton, Elaine S. (Elaine Schwartz), 1946– author.
Title: No ordinary women : making a difference through righteous influence /
Elaine S. Dalton.
Description: Salt Lake City, Utah : Deseret Book, [2016] | Includes bibliographical references and index.
Identifiers: LCCN 2016015244 | ISBN 9781629721514 (hardbound : alk. paper)
Subjects: LCSH: Women—Religious aspects—The Church of Jesus Christ of Latter-day Saints. | The Church of Jesus Christ of Latter-day Saints—Doctrines. | Mormon Church—Doctrines.
Classification: LCC BX8643.W66 D35 2016 | DDC 248.8/430882893—dc23
LC record available at https://lccn.loc.gov/2016015244

Printed in the United States of America
Publishers Printing, Salt Lake City, UT

10 9 8 7 6 5 4 3 2 1

To the incredible women all over the world who have come into my life and taught me that there are "no ordinary women."

To my magnificent mother, Emma Schwartz, my mother-in-law, Jessie Dalton, my daughter, Emi Edgley, and my daughters-in-law, Sheri, Amy, Kathy, Annie, and Lizzie, who are indeed "no ordinary women."

And to my precious granddaughters, who are well on their way to becoming extraordinary women:

Eliza
Ella
Louisa
Sarah
Rachel
Caroline
Annabel
Emily
Hannah
Alice
Emma
Esther
Charlotte
Claire

"My dear sisters, your Heavenly Father loves you—each of you. That love never changes. It is not influenced by your appearance, by your possessions, or by the amount of money you have in your bank account. It is not changed by your talents and abilities. It is simply there."

—PRESIDENT THOMAS S. MONSON

"We Never Walk Alone," *Ensign*, Nov. 2013, 123–24

Acknowledgments

First and foremost I express my eternal gratitude to my husband, Steve, for his love and devotion, for his encouragement and example, and for his loving kindness to me.

I also express my deep appreciation to Sheri Dew, who has mentored and believed in me. Also to Jana Erickson for helping me compile all my thoughts. To my editors, Tracy Keck and Emily Watts, I express my gratitude for their thorough work. And a big thank you to all at Deseret Book who have had a hand in making this expression of our Heavenly Father's love for His daughters all over the world a reality.

Contents

PART ONE

PART TWO

Part One

1

Act Well Thy Part

When I was in college, I auditioned for a group called the BYU International Folk Dancers. To my surprise, I got in! That summer our group had the unique privilege of touring the missions in Europe to help promote missionary work. It was a wonderful opportunity, but I have to admit that I went on the trip a little reluctantly. A few months earlier, my father had unexpectedly passed away at the age of forty-five. I was worried about leaving my mother, and I also didn't want to be the cause of any unnecessary expense for her. I tried to do the best I could, but it was a difficult summer for me.

While we were in Scotland, I felt especially alone and became discouraged. I couldn't concentrate. I wanted to quit and go home. We performed our show that night for members, investigators, and missionaries. After our performance we were invited to go to the mission home for dinner. As I walked there, I thought to myself, "You're not doing any good here, Elaine. You might as well just go home. You're not doing what you should be doing." As I proceeded up the walk, I saw a stone placed in a well-kept garden by the gate. Chiseled in the stone were the words, "What-e'er thou art, act well thy part."

At that moment, standing in front of the stone in that beautiful garden, I felt that heaven spoke to me. Those words went deeply into my heart. I stood in that garden with tears in my eyes. I felt like my father and my grandparents were there talking to me, and the message that came into my heart and

mind was powerful and clear. "You have a part to play. Don't minimize it. Your part matters because *you* matter!" That message changed me. I knew at that instant that I had a part to play not only on that dancing tour but throughout my life—and that it was very important to "act well" my part.

What-e'er thou art, act well thy part. That simple statement renewed my vision that Heavenly Father knew me and had a plan for my life, and the Spirit I felt helped me understand that my part, however small, mattered.

Later I learned that this saying had once motivated the prophet David O. McKay while he was serving as a young missionary in Scotland. He had seen this very stone on a building at a discouraging time on his mission, and the words lifted him. Years later, as the building was being torn down, he made arrangements to obtain the stone and had it placed in the garden at the mission home.

I also learned that every symbol in that stone has a different shape and size and that together they form what is called a magic square. Designed by John Allan, a nineteenth-century architect, each of the nine squares in the grid contains a different symbol or shape representing a numeric value. For example, the hand in the upper left corner, with its five fingers, represents the number five. No matter how you draw a straight line through any three shapes, the total always adds up to eighteen. But if any of the shapes are moved out of position, the equation does

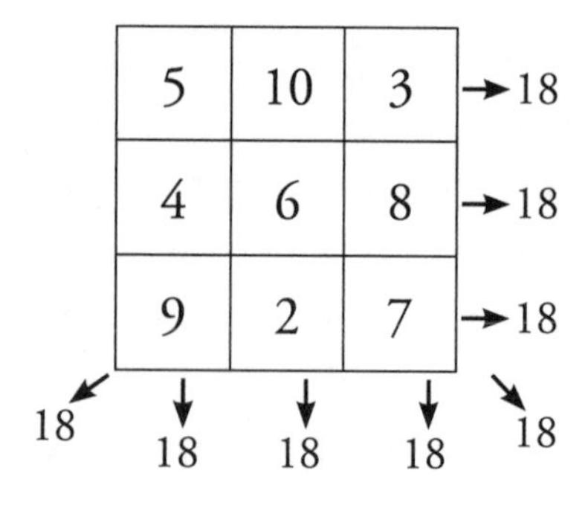

not work and the shapes will no longer add up correctly. So the symbols in the magic square also serve to say, "Act well [your] part." The stone's message is clear—each of us has an irreplaceable part to play.

These are magnificent times. This is the time that has been anticipated throughout eternity, and we *do* have an amazing part to play. As daughters of God, we are each unique and different in our circumstances and experiences, and our part matters because *we* matter. We are no ordinary women. We are elect, and each of us has a unique, divine mission to perform.

We learn more about what it means to be elect women in the vision of the redemption of the dead given to President Joseph F. Smith recorded in the Doctrine and Covenants. He relates that he saw many of the noble and great ones who had been on the earth prior to the Savior's coming, including our glorious Mother Eve. He also saw the Prophet Joseph Smith, Hyrum Smith, his father, and "*other choice spirits* who were reserved to come forth in the fulness of times to take part in laying the foundations of the great latter-day work" (D&C 138:53; emphasis added). Who were those other choice spirits? Our generation was somewhere there among those "noble and great" leaders, prepared in the world of the spirits to be on the earth at this time! The scriptures tell us that "even before [we] were born, [we], *with many others*, received [our] first lessons in the world of spirits and were prepared to come forth in the due time of the Lord to labor in his vineyard for the salvation of the souls of men" (D&C 138:55–56; emphasis added).

As daughters of God, we are each unique and different in our circumstances and experiences, and our part matters because we matter.

You and I have been prepared and reserved to be here on the earth now, uniquely positioned in time and place to make a difference, to contribute and lead in such a way that our righteous influence will change the world. I know it is possible. Our opportunities for leadership and service abound not only in our families, our neighborhoods, our communities, and in the Church, but in the world as well.

Each of us came to the earth with gifts and talents to help us accomplish our part. And we know from scripture that each of us has come with at least *one* gift. We are also instructed in scripture to seek and even "covet earnestly the best gifts" (1 Corinthians 12:31; see also D&C 46:8) so that we can assist in building the kingdom here on the earth.

You are not ordinary. You were custom made—physically, spiritually, and mentally—to fulfill your divine mission, and you have been given an enhanced ability to influence others through the gift of the Holy Ghost. And yet your part will not be easy. Our daily contributions of nurturing, teaching, and caring for others may seem mundane, diminished, difficult, and even demeaning at times. There will be trials and tribulations in abundance, but remember that the Lord has stated and promised, "And the saints also shall hardly escape; nevertheless, I, the Lord, am with them" (D&C 63:34).

Throughout history we have examples of extraordinary women who acted well their part, despite challenging circumstances. Mother Eve made a difficult and yet intelligent, informed, and inspired choice in the Garden of Eden. Had she failed to act well her part, none of us would be here! Mary had an amazing part to play as the mother of our Savior. She said, "Be it unto me according to thy word" (Luke 1:38). Mary is a wonderful example of fulfilling her unique, divine mission in life as she humbly submitted to God's will.

Esther also had a part to play. Her life was not easy. Both her parents died, leaving her an orphan. She was sent to another country to live with her uncle Mordecai. In my mind, I think the

Lord used her uniqueness—her unique looks—and even moved her to another land where she could play the unique part that she was given to play. Because of her courage in acting well a part only she could play, the entire Jewish nation was saved.

> "Very often I feel like a little pencil in God's Hands. He does the writing, He does the thinking, He does the movement, I have only to be the pencil."
>
> —MOTHER TERESA

Joan of Arc was a peasant girl who believed that God had chosen her to lead France to independence from English domination. She lost her life acting well her part. Mother Teresa changed the world and earned the honorary title of "mother" even though she never married or physically bore children. But she mothered the poorest of the poor in India after experiencing what she termed "the call within." She said, "Very often I feel like a little pencil in God's Hands. He does the writing, He does the thinking, He does the movement, I have only to be the pencil" (Brian Kolodiejchuk, *Mother Teresa: Come Be My Light: The Private Writings of the Saint of Calcutta* [2007], 363). She too acted her part well.

Emily Dickinson, one of my favorite American poets, echoed the feelings each of us may have from time to time. She wrote, "I'm Nobody! Who are you? Are you—Nobody—too?" She spoke so clearly and plainly and pointed out through her poetry that the simple things matter and that even though we may feel we are "nobody," we do in fact have a special, specific, and unique contribution to make. Emily Dickinson did not see success during her lifetime, but she is now considered to be a master poetess. And her simple poetry inspires all who read it.

Another woman who made a difference in the world is Rosa Parks. I don't know what motivated Rosa Parks, but this I do know: one day while riding the bus, she thought, "I have an identity. I am a daughter of God." She refused to sit at the back of the bus, and she changed the world with that courageous decision.

Sara Blakely invented Spanx. I don't know about you, but she's changed my world! Today Sara Blakely has a billion-dollar business. As she was growing up, her father encouraged his children to try something challenging each day. Every evening at dinner he went around the table and asked each of his children, "What did you fail at today?" And then he asked, "And what did you learn from your failure?" Sara Blakely was raised with the idea that failure is not a bad thing, but a pattern that eventually leads to success. She used her failed attempts to improve and try again, and she too has changed the world (or at least mine!).

Last, but not at all least, is my mother, Emma Schwartz, who became a widow at age forty-five, who taught school, raised our family, and made it possible for each one of us to have a college education. Why? So that we could act well our parts and be prepared to be contributors. My mother's part was never celebrated, it wasn't known by the world, but she changed *my* world. Because she was faithful and a covenant keeper, our family was blessed during those difficult years, and because of her faith in the Lord, her strict obedience to the commandments, and her pure love and example, we still are blessed today.

Each one of us has a part to play, and no matter how small or how insignificant we think our part is, it matters to the Lord. It matters to the whole. It matters because *we* matter. Together we have something very important—and unique to each of us—to do.

Emma Schwartz

2

He Knows Us

It was "on the morning of a beautiful, clear day, early in the spring of eighteen hundred and twenty" when fourteen-year-old Joseph Smith went into the grove, knelt in prayer, and "saw two Personages, whose brightness and glory defy all description, standing above [him] in the air." He said: "One of them spake unto me, *calling me by name* and said, pointing to the other—*This is My Beloved Son. Hear Him!*" (Joseph Smith—History 1:14, 17; emphasis added). Can you imagine how fourteen-year-old Joseph must have felt to see God the Father and His Son, Jesus Christ, and to hear Heavenly Father call him by his name?

When I visited the Sacred Grove, I tried to imagine what it must have been like to be Joseph Smith. In those quiet moments, the Spirit whispered to my beating heart that I was standing on holy ground and that all that the Prophet Joseph Smith related after that sacred experience was and is true. Then came the powerful realization that we are all the beneficiaries of his faith, courage, and steadfast desire to obey God. He had received an answer to his humble prayer. He had seen the Father and His Beloved Son. There in the Sacred Grove, I knew that Heavenly Father not only knew Joseph Smith by name, but He also knows each of us by name. And just as Joseph Smith had an important part to play in this great and marvelous work of the Restoration, we too have an important part to play in these latter days.

Did you know that Heavenly Father knows you personally—by name? The scriptures teach us that this is true. When Enos went into the woods to pray, he recorded, "There came a voice unto me, saying: *Enos*, thy sins are forgiven thee, and thou shalt be blessed" (Enos 1:5; emphasis added). Likewise, Moses not only prayed but also talked to God face to face, and God said to Moses, "I have a work for thee, *Moses*, my son" (Moses 1:6; emphasis added). The Lord knew Jacob's name and changed it to *Israel* to more accurately reflect his unique mission on the earth (see Bible Dictionary, "Israel," 708). Similarly, He changed the names of Paul and Abraham and Sarah (see Acts 13:9; Genesis 17:5, 15). In Doctrine and Covenants, section 25, Emma Smith is given a blessing for her comfort and guidance in life. The Lord begins this blessing by saying, "Hearken unto the voice of the Lord your God, while I speak unto you, *Emma Smith*, my daughter" (D&C 25:1; emphasis added).

You may not have heard the Lord call you by name, but He knows each one of you and He knows your name! Elder Neal A. Maxwell said: "I testify to you that God has known you individually . . . for a long, long time (see D&C 93:23). He has loved you for a long, long time. He not only knows the names of all the stars (see Ps. 147:4, Isa. 40:26); He knows your names and all your heartaches and your joys!" ("Remember How Merciful the Lord Hath Been," *Ensign*, May 2004, 46).

"God has known you individually . . . for a long, long time."

—ELDER NEAL A. MAXWELL

How can you know that your name and needs are known by our Heavenly Father? Elder Robert D. Hales counseled: "Turn to the scriptures. Kneel in prayer. Ask in faith. Listen to the Holy Ghost. . . . Live the gospel with patience and persistence" ("Receiving a Testimony of the Restored Gospel of Jesus Christ," *Ensign*, Nov. 2003, 31).

That's what Joseph did. His testimony helps all of us know that we are known and loved by our Heavenly Father. Joseph Smith's history provides an important pattern for each of us. Have you ever had a problem and not known what to do? Joseph said: "My mind was called up to serious reflection and great uneasiness. . . . I often said to myself: What is to be done?" (JS—H 1:8, 10). Joseph studied the scriptures, pondered their promises, and then "came to the determination to 'ask of God'" (JS—H 1:13). The answer he received that beautiful spring day changed his life and direction. He knew! He gained a testimony of God and Jesus Christ, and his testimony enabled him to live the gospel with patience and persistence.

We can apply the same teachings Joseph did when we don't know what to do, when we are overwhelmed, when we feel surrounded by temptation, or when we feel unworthy or alone. We can pray! We can call upon God in the name of His Holy Son, Jesus Christ, and seek comfort, guidance, and direction.

Joseph keenly realized his imperfections and weaknesses. Again—he prayed. In response to this prayer, the angel Moroni visited him. Joseph recounted: "*He called me by name*" and said "that God had a work for me to do" (JS—H 1:33; emphasis added). As we pray, the Lord will also guide and prepare us to do our part.

When I was a teenager and my father became very ill, I prayed constantly and asked Heavenly Father to bless my father to get well. He was in the hospital for one month, and then he unexpectedly passed away.

This was a tragedy for our family. To us it didn't make any

sense, because we needed our father. I prayed to understand why this had happened and why Heavenly Father hadn't answered my prayers. It felt to me like the heavens were silent. I didn't get an answer to my prayers. I felt that Heavenly Father had left me all alone. But I persisted and continued to pray.

When you trust in the Lord, you can do anything—even if it is really hard—because He *does* direct your path.

A year later I attended a sacrament meeting where the speaker read a scripture from Proverbs: "Trust in the Lord with all thine heart; and lean not unto thine own understanding. In all thy ways acknowledge him, and he shall direct thy paths" (Proverbs 3:5–6).

And as those words were spoken, the Spirit witnessed to me that this was the answer to my prayer! I simply needed to trust the Lord—to have faith in Him. It took a long time to receive that answer, and it wasn't the one that I had wanted, but it was a wonderful answer to all of my prayers. I wasn't supposed to understand why this happened. I was supposed to trust in the Lord.

I have learned that when you trust in the Lord, you *can* do anything—even if it is really hard—because He *does* direct your path. He'll walk by your side. He'll hold your hand.

He will send His angels to surround you. He will enable you through the power of His infinite Atonement. That's my testimony. And it is true for each of us.

Every one of us will experience adversity. We may not always understand the Lord's design for our lives, but we are never alone. He is ever with us, and He promises us, "Ye cannot behold with your natural eyes, for the present time, the design of your God concerning those things which shall come hereafter, and the glory which shall follow after much tribulation" (D&C 58:3).

We may not always understand the Lord's design for our lives, but we are never alone. He is ever with us.

What does the Lord expect us to do? He expects us to press forward. He expects us to play our part valiantly in the final scenes prior to His coming. He expects us to prove ourselves worthy to return and live with Him. He expects us to become like Him.

I love the words in the hymn "Joseph Smith's First Prayer": "But undaunted, still he trusted / In his Heav'nly Father's care" (*Hymns of The Church of Jesus Christ of Latter-day Saints* [1985], no. 26). To be *undaunted* means unshaken in purpose, resolutely courageous. Joseph described himself as a "disturber" of the adversary's kingdom. He said, "It seems as though the adversary was aware . . . that I was destined to prove a disturber and an annoyer of his kingdom" (JS—H 1:20). I have written in the margin of my scriptures, "*Be a disturber!*" Each of us can trust in our Heavenly Father's care.

Each of us will play an important part if we follow the pattern established by Joseph Smith. The Lord strengthened Joseph Smith for his divine mission. He will strengthen you for yours. He may even send His holy angels to tutor you. Now the challenge is this: Will you be in such a place that angels can enter? Will you be still enough to hear? Will you be undaunted and trust?

Winston Churchill said: "To every [woman] there comes . . . that special moment when [she] is figuratively tapped on the shoulder and offered the chance to do a special thing, unique to [her] and fitted to [her] talent. What a tragedy if that moment finds [her] unprepared or unqualified for the work which would be [her] finest hour."

I believe that you and I are being tapped on the shoulder. These are not ordinary times, and you are not ordinary women. You are daughters of our Heavenly Father. Each of you has a part to play in this great and marvelous work. The Savior will help you. He will lead you by the hand (see D&C 112:10; Abraham 1:18). I testify that He knows you by name.

3

The Influence of a Righteous Woman

Speaking to the women of the Church nearly a century ago, President Joseph F. Smith said: "It is not for you to be led by the women of the world; it is for you to lead the . . . women of the world, in everything that is praise-worthy, everything that is God-like, everything that is uplifting and . . . purifying to the children of men" (*Teachings of Presidents of the Church: Joseph F. Smith* [1998], 184).

We are daughters of God. We are not ordinary women. We were born to be leaders. Yet the world would make you think that you are insignificant or that there is a certain mold you have to fit. And, according to the world, if you don't fit that mold, you really can't have any influence and you really aren't of any worth. That is an absolute lie. Every one of us on the earth today has been reserved to be here now during the winding-up scenes in preparation for the Savior's Second Coming. We have been prepared and chosen and reserved to be here now, and that is a divine compliment.

We are not here to sit back and be passive. We are here to lead. Moroni talks about us in the Book of Mormon. He even calls to us, saying, "Awake, and arise from the dust, O Jerusalem; yea, and put on thy beautiful garments, O daughter of Zion; and strengthen thy stakes and enlarge thy borders" (Moroni 10:31). Enlarge your borders of friendship. Enlarge your service. Enlarge your circle of influence. Live a purposeful life, not a passive life. Arise!

There is nothing in this world as personal, as nurturing, or as life-changing as the influence of a righteous woman.

There is nothing in this world as personal, as nurturing, or as life-changing as the influence of a righteous woman. There is no responsibility of greater importance than to love, nurture, teach, guide, and *mother* the next generation.

When my mother was in her teens, her mother—my Grandmother Martin—suffered a series of strokes that left her paralyzed and unable to speak. My mother assumed her mother's role of cooking, cleaning, and caring for her father and her three brothers, along with attending school. She also cared lovingly for her mother each day.

This situation must have been very difficult, and the additional responsibilities she had to assume at such an early age must have been hard to bear. But I am told that my mother never complained and was patient and kind to her mother, father, and brothers. She did not let her circumstances discourage her or excuse her from achieving her goals and dreams. In fact, she continued to attend school and gain further education. When she graduated from high school, she was given an award for never having missed a day of school in twelve years. She was never tardy, and she had also earned the highest grades possible in all her classes.

After her graduation, my mother attended college in a city several miles away. Each weekend she returned home to care for her mother. She changed the bed linens, did the washing, cleaned the house, and prepared meals for the week for her family and then returned to school on Monday morning. When she met and married my father, they moved into her parents' home so that she could continue to care for her mother. I was raised in that home and still carry with me the memories of my mother's service and sacrifice. My life has been richly blessed because of her example.

Because of my mother's attitude, I always thought it was a privilege to live with my grandparents. I came to know them in a way I could never have known them otherwise. I loved my Grandmother Martin dearly, and even though she could not speak, I knew she loved me by the look in her eyes. I learned how to read on her lap. She was always there and was never too busy to listen to me. Her attitude was one of cheer and optimism. She was grateful for the smallest things. She loved it when I helped her walk around the living room, and she loved to go for a ride in the car. She blessed my life as a young child and still today as an adult.

Both my mother and my grandmother were talented, educated, capable women. I am sure this circumstance and trial was not what my grandmother had envisioned for her life, nor was it what my mother had had in mind for her life. But their example changed me—they changed *my* world.

A few years ago my magnificent ninety-two-year-old mother passed away. She left this mortal existence as she had lived—quietly. Her life was not what she had planned. After her husband, my father, passed away when he was forty-five, leaving her with three children—me and my two brothers—she lived forty-seven years as a widow. Because of the priority she placed on education, she was able to support our family by teaching school during the day and teaching piano lessons at night. She cared for her aging father, my grandfather, who then lived next door. She made sure that each of us received a college education. In fact, she insisted on it so that we could be "contributors."

I remember going home one weekend after my father passed away during my first year at Brigham Young University, where I was enrolled, and telling my mother that I was planning to drop out, come home, and get a job to help support our family. My mother replied, "Oh, no, you won't. You will go back to BYU and you will graduate, even if I have to take in laundry, and you will make your father and me proud." I knew she meant it, and I knew she was right.

Before I married my husband, Steve, my mother made me promise I would still graduate from BYU, and she made my husband promise he would help make it possible. I graduated with a degree in English, a secondary teaching certificate, and a minor in speech and dramatic arts—and expecting our first child.

Clearly my mother knew the importance of getting an education, but she also knew some things that are not often talked about today. She taught by example that the home is a cottage industry, and educated women have amazing influence in their homes, communities, and, yes, in the world. And through my own experience, I have learned that an education will make us "more fit for the kingdom" (*Hymns*, no. 131) and will be used in ways we may not anticipate. I cannot tell you how many times I bowed my head and thanked my Father

> The home is a cottage industry, and educated women have amazing influence in their homes, communities, and, yes, in the world.

in Heaven for my education as I served the Lord as Young Women general president. I have used my education every single day.

Some would say I never used my education because I have never taught school. But they are wrong! I have used it as a mother and grandmother (starting with poems, lullabies, and bedtime stories), as a wife, helping my husband finish his MBA (reading his papers, editing and correcting grammar and spelling), and in Church service. When my husband—a successful salesman for a medical company—was replaced by four younger, lower-commissioned reps, I used my education to help make ends meet while my husband was determining his next steps. I started a small interior design company that helped make ends meet for a time while my husband decided which career path to pursue.

I believe the experience of starting and running my own company prepared me for my service as the Young Women general president. I learned public relations skills, accounting, billing procedures, spreadsheets, computer skills, purchasing processes, how to establish accounts, sales and presentation skills, how to present in a boardroom, and so much more.

The fact is that mothers are the CEOs of a world-changing organization: the family and the home. Motherhood is the most important as well as the most challenging job anyone will ever assume.

All my life I have been passionate about the role of motherhood. I feel and have always felt that I could impact the world more by being a good mother and raising a righteous, qualified family than through anything else I could do. And fortunately I have been blessed with my heart's desire, but that does not count out those women who are single by any means. As Barbara Bush, the wife of former United States President George H. W. Bush once told the graduating class at Wellesley College: "Your success as a family . . . our success as a society . . . depends *not* on what happens at the White House, but on what happens inside your house" (Barbara Bush, *A Memoir,* [1994], 540).

Mothers are the CEOs of a world-changing organization: the family and the home.

I believe that if a woman can manage an efficient, organized, Spirit-filled home, whether married with children or single, she can do almost anything. I believe it is in the home that we learn discipline, communication skills, interpersonal skills, negotiation skills, how to compromise, and how to multitask. It is in the home that we learn scheduling skills, management skills, public relations skills, budgeting, conscious consumerism, goal setting, and interpersonal relationship skills. It is in a home setting that we learn fairness, values, ethics, and long-range planning, and so many more things. And the Lord outlines the pattern to follow in Doctrine and Covenants 109: "Establish a house, even a house of prayer, a house of fasting, a house of faith, a house of learning, a house of glory, a house of order, a house of God" (D&C 109:8).

Of all women, both married and single, President Gordon B. Hinckley once said: "We must never lose sight of the strength of the women. . . . It is mothers who most directly affect the lives of their children. . . . It is mothers who nurture them and bring them up in the ways of the Lord. Their influence is paramount. . . . They are the creators of life. They are the nurturers of children. They are the teachers of young women. They are our indispensable companions. They are our co-workers in building the kingdom of God. How great is their role, how marvelous their contribution" ("Standing Strong and Immovable," *Worldwide Leadership Training Meeting*, Jan. 10, 2004, 21). And as Sheri Dew so appropriately asked in the title of one of her talks, "Are we not all mothers?" (*Ensign*, Nov. 2001, 96–98).

We can never measure the extent of our influence as righteous women. A few years ago my daughter-in-law Annie went to her family home to pack its contents. Her mother had passed away just one month after Annie married our son Jess.

We can never measure the extent of our influence as righteous women.

She was heartbroken. She later told me how hard it had been. Her remark was, "How do you pack up a life and put its contents in little boxes and distribute it to whomever?"

My response was, "You don't. You only pack *things*. Life goes on in the evidence, and the evidence is *you*. It is your life well lived. It is your example. It is carrying on the things your mother taught you and honoring your heritage and legacy by making honorable and good choices. It is pressing forward. It is maintaining 'a perfect brightness of hope' (2 Nephi 31:20). It is passing on all that your mother taught you. Her life is not in a box." It is really true—the lives of mothers and righteous, covenant-keeping women influence and bless generations.

We are mothers whether we have children in our home or not. We can be mothers to others' children and nurture and warn and protect and love them, too. Who knows what our influence might do? I invite you to look around. Who needs to hear you call them by name? Who needs you and your influence? Who needs your healing, nurturing touch? Who needs someone to understand them and to believe in them? Who needs to hear you say, "Everything will be all right," or "I just know you can do it," or "I love you"? If we really want to make a difference, it will happen as we mother our own children and those others who need us.

My mother never complained about her lot in life. She went forward, keeping her covenants, and because she did, she called down the powers of heaven to bless our home and to send miracles. She relied on the power of prayer, priesthood, and covenant promises. She was faithful in her service to the Lord. Her steadfast devotion steadied us, her children. She often repeated the scripture: "I, the Lord, am bound when ye do what I say; but when ye do not what I say, ye have no promise" (D&C 82:10). That was her motto, and she knew it was true. She understood what it meant to be a covenant keeper. She was never recognized by the world. She didn't want that. She recognized and understood who she was and *whose* she was—a daughter of God. Indeed, it can be said of our mother that she acted well her part.

I agree with Elder M. Russell Ballard when he stated: "Popular culture today often makes women look silly, inconsequential, mindless, and powerless. It objectifies them and disrespects them and then suggests that they are able to leave their mark on mankind only by seduction—easily the most pervasively dangerous message the adversary sends to women about themselves" ("Mothers and Daughters," *Ensign*, May 2010, 19).

In contrast, President Spencer W. Kimball declared: "No greater recognition can come to you in this world than to be known as a woman of God. No greater status can be conferred upon you than being a daughter of God who experiences true sisterhood, wifehood, and motherhood, or other tasks which influence lives for good." He continued, "Much of the major growth that is coming to the Church in the last days . . . will happen to the degree that the women of the Church reflect righteousness and articulateness in their lives and to the degree that the women of the Church are seen as distinct and different—in happy ways—from the women of the world" ("The Role of Righteous Women," *Ensign*, Nov. 1979, 102–4).

> "No greater recognition can come to you in this world than to be known as a woman of God."
>
> —PRESIDENT SPENCER W. KIMBALL

You were born to lead the world, not to be led by the world. And if you desire to make a difference in the world, you must be different from the world. We have been reserved to be on the earth now when the trials and the temptations are the greatest but also when the opportunities and the blessings abound for our individual and combined power of righteous influence.

Remember, "by small and simple things are great things brought to pass" (Alma 37:6).

Here are some ideas of small and simple ways you can become the extraordinary woman the Lord knows and loves.

REFLECT:

- How do you know you are a daughter of our Heavenly Father and that He loves and knows you?
- What examples have you witnessed of women acting well their parts?
- What evidence testifies that the Lord knows you personally?
- When have you or your family been blessed by the influence of a righteous woman?
- Could it be that adversity strengthens and sometimes positions you to act well your part?

COMMIT:

- Spend some time pondering, even writing down the parts that you are currently called to play—big or small or in between.

- Be undaunted in your trust in the Lord. Draw near unto Him so that He can draw even nearer unto you (see D&C 88:63).
- View yourself as a leader among women. Make a list of the spheres where you can have a righteous influence—your family, your workplace, your children's schools, your ward, your book group, your local government. Where else?

ACT:

- Read your patriarchal blessing and list the gifts you've been given.
- Make a list of gifts you need now or would like to develop.
- Choose a spiritual gift you would like to develop that will help you "act well thy part." Study this gift, pray for this gift, and go out each day trusting that the Lord will bless you with this gift.
- Make note of the ways you see your spiritual gifts enabling you to be a righteous leader. Express gratitude for the gifts you've been given, and try to recognize spiritual gifts in others.
- Be a disturber! Find a way each day to frustrate the goals of the adversary. Turn off an inappropriate show or compliment someone who believes she doesn't have value. Record in your journal or share with your family the daily victories the Lord enables you to accomplish.

Part Two

4

We Can Do Hard Things

From 1983 to 1991, an annual race was held in Australia between two major cities. The route of the Westfield Sydney to Melbourne Ultramarathon stretched 543.7 miles (875 kilometers) and took runners five days to complete. Naturally, the grueling race was typically attempted by elite athletes who trained for months or years in preparation for the event. Most were under thirty years of age and were in top physical shape.

The first year of the race, a sixty-one-year-old man named Cliff Young showed up wearing overalls and work boots. Everyone assumed he was there as a spectator, and they were shocked when he announced that he was there to compete.

Members of the press, other competitors, and spectators alike were extremely skeptical. They thought there was no way an old man wearing work boots and overalls instead of expensive running gear could finish such a race.

But Cliff was confident. When questioned, he explained that he had grown up on a farm without horses or tractors. When storms would roll in, Cliff's job was to go out and round up the sheep. His family had 2,000 sheep spread out over 2,000 acres. Cliff explained that he sometimes had to run after those sheep for two or three days before he'd rounded them all up. With that experience under his belt, he truly believed he could finish the race.

When the race started, Cliff was quickly left in the dust. Many spectators couldn't help but laugh at Cliff because he didn't even run properly; instead he had a slow, lumbering shuffle. Some even feared for his physical well-being and safety in such a test of endurance.

But Cliff had a surprise up his sleeve. Unlike all the young, professional athletes, Cliff hadn't trained to run for about eighteen hours each day of the race and then sleep the remaining six hours. In fact, he wasn't even aware that was the standard training and racing schedule. When everyone else awoke to begin the second day of the race, they were shocked to find out that not only was Cliff still in the race, but he had run all through the night!

The press and spectators eventually asked Cliff about his plans for finishing the race. To their amazement, Cliff stated simply that he would just keep running until the race was over, without ever stopping to sleep, just as he did when he rounded up the 2,000 sheep before a storm.

And that is exactly what he did. Each day of the race he gained momentum and got closer to the leading racers, who were all taking breaks to sleep. By the last day, he had run past all of the young, elite athletes. He was the very first competitor to cross the finish line. That day Cliff Young showed the world that a slow, old farmer wearing overalls and work boots could achieve what seemed impossible.

Adding even more charm to the story, Cliff was completely surprised when he was awarded $10,000 for winning the race. He explained that he'd had no idea there even was a prize and that it had not been his reason for entering. Since he had never cared about the money in the first place, instead of keeping it, Cliff divided up his winnings among several of the other runners.

Besides becoming a beloved figure in Australian history, Cliff Young has left a legacy among ultramarathon runners. His "Young Shuffle" has been put to use by many racers who have found it to be more energy efficient. At least three other champions of the Westfield Sydney to Melbourne Ultramarathon used the "Cliff Young Shuffle" to ultimately win the race. Perhaps his greatest influence on the race, though, was the precedent he set for not sleeping at all throughout the run. Once Cliff showed that it could be done, all other would-be race winners were required to step up their training and learn to run the full distance without sleeping, just as Cliff Young did.

What does this story teach us? We can set the standard! We can endure! We can do more than we think we can! We can do hard things! We can change the world! Remember that you were born to be different from the world and to make a difference in the world, so believe in yourself and don't be afraid to be you.

What I have learned and know is that anything worth doing is not easy and that we can do anything that is not easy if we prepare well and believe in ourselves. You may not be contemplating a marathon or an ultramarathon, but you may be in the middle of a challenge that feels like one. You may feel opposed on every side. You may wonder if you really can continue to "press forward with . . . a perfect brightness of hope" (2 Nephi 31:20) as the Apostle Paul said to his young friend Timothy, "Cast not away therefore your confidence, which hath great recompense of reward" (Hebrews 10:35). Go forward with faith knowing that if you do your part, the Lord will always do His. He will strengthen us.

We must be courageous enough to be *different* from the world. We must be willing to lead!

We must be courageous enough to be different from the world. We must be willing to lead! We must and can have the faith and courage to confront challenges and make right decisions. We must be willing and prepared to be articulate advocates for the restored gospel of Jesus Christ. And because we are covenant keepers, we *can* do hard things.

It is an interesting thing that as human beings, we seek comfort zones. Based on everything I read in the scriptures, I don't think the Lord likes us to be in a comfort zone. He repeatedly takes His choicest disciples out of their comfort zones and challenges them by their circumstances, their trials, and their opportunities to become more and to do more.

Certainly many women in the scriptures confronted challenging circumstances in their families, in their society, and personally. Such was the case with Jochebed, who placed her newborn son, Moses, in a basket in the bulrushes to hide him and save his life from an edict by the pharaoh to exterminate all Hebrew male children. What seemed like a desperate circumstance worked for her good, and her precious son was found by the queen, who adopted him as her own. Jochebed was employed to be her own son's wet nurse. Because of his mother's faith and courage, Moses was raised in the palace of the pharaoh and later led his nation out of bondage. It all started with one courageous woman who was inspired to do a very hard thing and did it with full faith.

The daughters of Onitah aren't spoken of often. Their names are not even mentioned in scripture, but their father must have been an important man as a royal descendant of Ham and one who held the priesthood. These three young women would not give in to the moral climate of their day. The scriptural account states that they "were offered up because of their virtue; they would not bow down to worship gods of wood or of stone" (Abraham 1:11). They stood their ground. They knew that God had the power to save them, but even if He didn't, their commitment and resolve would remain unchanged because they understood their identity and they had testimonies. They were true to their beliefs and were sacrificed on the altar.

Their story parallels others in scriptural writ, including that of three young men who also refused to worship false gods. Elder Neal A. Maxwell observed: "Matching those three young men [Shadrach, Meshach, and Abednego] are three young women whose names we do not have. They are mentioned in the book of Abraham, remarkable young women about whom I am anxious to know more. . . . Some day the faithful will get to meet them" (Neal A. Maxwell, *Not My Will, But Thine* [1988], 120).

As I stated before, Esther was another young woman who learned to face challenges and trials with courage long before she displayed the courage to go before the king. Her life preparation came in the form of difficult challenges that served to strengthen her and help her understand her identity. Who knows but that we each have "come to the kingdom for such a time as this" (Esther 4:14) and are even now being polished by our challenges?

We each have an opportunity to shape the future, to promote and exemplify moral values, to advocate for traditional families, and to defend the right to express religious convictions. Within our grasp is the opportunity to do something extraordinary for individuals, society, and the nation. We are uniquely positioned in a changing and challenging time to serve others and contribute in such a way that our righteous influence will literally change the world.

Who knows but that we each have "come to the kingdom for such a time as this" and are even now being polished by our challenges?

We must go forward with full confidence. Did you know that the word *confidence* is derived from the Latin words *con* and *fideo*, which means *with faith*? Confidence requires faith and purity. That is why Peter admonishes all to "add to [our] faith virtue; and to virtue knowledge" (2 Peter 1:5). Our faith and virtue qualify us for the companionship of the Holy Ghost, who will "show unto [us] all things what [we] should do" (2 Nephi 32:5). That is sure knowledge and assured success.

The Lord also instructed us to "let virtue garnish [our] thoughts unceasingly" and promised that "then shall [our] confidence wax strong in the presence of God" and "the Holy Ghost shall be [our] constant companion" (D&C 121:45–46).

Several years ago, my husband and I were in Nauvoo. When I'm in Nauvoo, I love getting up early in the morning and running those streets in silence, thinking and pondering about what it must have been like to be in Nauvoo at that time when the Church was just young. Always I am touched as I read the inscriptions from pioneer journals that have been reproduced on plaques placed along Parley Street. One of those that always touches me is taken from something Bathsheba Smith wrote in her journal just before leaving Nauvoo. She said, "My last act in that precious spot was to tidy the rooms, sweep up the floor, and set the broom in its accustomed place behind the door. Then with emotions in my heart . . . I gently closed the door and faced an unknown future, faced it with faith in God" ("The Trail of Hope: Exodus from Nauvoo," *Ensign*, July 2013, 42). In other words, she left that home, knowing that she'd never come back to it again, but she still left it beautiful. And then she wrote, "I walked out the door, into an unknown future." So many of those extraordinary men and women did just that. They gave

"I gently closed the door and faced an unknown future, faced it with faith in God."

—BATHSHEBA SMITH

up everything because they had faith in the Lord and the power of their covenants. They knew the gospel was true.

My husband had a lot of relatives in Nauvoo at the time of those faithful Saints. One of them was Zina Huntington, who later became general president of the Relief Society. As a young woman, she lived in upstate New York when the missionaries came and left a copy of the Book of Mormon for the family to read. When Zina first held that book in her hands, she said, "This is the truth, truth, truth!" ("How I Gained My Testimony of the Truth," *The Young Woman's Journal,* Apr. 1893, 318). She was converted to the gospel before she ever opened the Book of Mormon. She knew by the Spirit that it was a true record, and so she and her family left their beautiful two-story rock home in New York to move with the Saints to Kirtland, and then to Nauvoo, and later traveled west across the plains to the Salt Lake Valley. She was able to make a tough decision and face difficult challenges because of her faith and testimony and because of the power of her temple covenants. And as I go down Parley Street and read those inscriptions, I weep every time because I feel the spirit of those women there still and I acknowledge the sacrifices they made for us to be where we are now. Their faith changed our world!

While living in Nauvoo, Zina married and was expecting a baby. In that condition, she left her home, crossed the Mississippi River, and got just a little farther west before she had that baby on the banks of a river. The river was named Chariton, so the baby was named Chariton. I think about those kinds of hardships and sacrifices, and then I consider what we've been asked to do. And I think, "Oh, what we're doing is easy compared to what they did." But you know what? It's not. What we're doing now is pivotal. And it's not easy, and it's not going to get easier. In fact, I think it may get harder for us. And I think that we are going to have to be very strong and firm. We too are going to need to be converted. We're going to have to be like Zina and know that "this is the truth, truth, truth." So as I think about making a difference, I think about those women. How did they do it? What helped them? I believe it's all about having a testimony of Jesus Christ and *doing* what we know is true. That means acting upon our faith and knowledge, because "faith without works is dead" (James 2:26). And I believe our testimonies of Jesus Christ and His restored gospel will help us meet any of life's challenges.

Our testimonies of Jesus Christ and His restored gospel will help us meet any of life's challenges.

Our journey sometimes takes us on unexpected paths. There are twists and turns in the road that none of us can anticipate, and sometimes the path is uphill all the way. But with each of these twists and turns there is also opportunity—opportunity to choose our response and our plan of action.

President Monson said it best: "There is no resting place along the path called faithfulness. The trek is constant, and no lingering is allowed" ("Happiness—the Universal Quest," *Ensign*, Oct. 1993, 4).

One day my husband and I were running together, which is usually not a good idea because I am competitive and he is faster than I am. We started up a hill, and I was elated because running hills sometimes gives me an advantage. But this day, Steve ran like a gazelle, with ease, and I soon found myself way behind, in complete oxygen debt. Not wanting to be outdone, I called out, "I will meet you at the car." And I turned around and started back down the hill. To my surprise, Steve came alongside me and grabbed my hand and said, "Elaine, don't quit now. We are almost to the top of this hill. I'll run with you. And besides, Elaine, haven't you learned by now that you never make a decision to quit or turn back when you are on a hill?" So I pushed forward, and when we reached the top, I enjoyed the exquisite view and the elation of knowing I could do hard things—and, of course, the long downhill run to the car!

That day I learned an important life lesson. Never make a decision to turn back when you are on a hill. Since then I have learned to look at hills as opportunities.

I've also learned that at some point in this marathon of life, we are all bound to stumble. When that happens, remember that there is no such thing as failure. It is just life trying to move you in another direction. Feel bad for a moment, but then learn from every mistake. Every experience is there to teach you and move you into being more of who you really are—perhaps to strengthen and prepare you.

Difficulties in life can be opportunities to help us draw closer to the Savior and to trust in Him more fully.

Theodore Roosevelt wisely stated: "It is not the critic who counts; not the man who points out how the strong man stumbles, or where the doer of deeds could have done them better. The credit belongs to the man who is actually in the arena, whose face is marred by dust and sweat and blood; who strives valiantly; who errs, who comes short again and again, because there is no effort without error and shortcoming; but who does actually strive to do the deeds; who knows great enthusiasms, the great devotions; who spends himself in a worthy cause; who at the best knows in the end the triumph of high achievement, and who at the worst, if he fails, at least fails while daring greatly, so that his place shall never be with those cold and timid souls who neither know victory nor defeat" ("Citizenship in a Republic" [speech given at the Sorbonne in Paris, France], Apr. 23, 1910).

Difficulties in life can be opportunities to help us draw closer to the Savior and to trust in Him more fully. In the process of living close to Him each day, we develop Christlike attributes and qualities. And when we feel too weak to carry our burdens, we can look to the Savior for our strength.

On our mortal journey, trials are inevitable. They are designed to help us grow and progress. In such times, we press forward with faith in our Savior Jesus Christ, knowing that as we trust in Him, He shall direct our paths (see Proverbs 3:5–6). I believe that is why Ammon testified, "Yea, I know that I am nothing; as to my strength I am weak; therefore I will not boast of myself, but I will boast of my God, for in his strength I can do *all* things" (Alma 26:12; emphasis added).

And truly, in the strength of His infinite Atonement, we can and will be enabled to do hard things. This I know!

5

We Are Led by the Spirit

On the desk in my office, I have a bronze replica of a sculpture of a young woman whose name is Kristina. The original life-sized sculpture of Kristina stands on a pier in Copenhagen, Denmark, positioned so that she is looking out over the sea toward Zion. Her decision to join the Church and leave her home was not an easy one, and you can see that the opposing winds are blowing fiercely against her. She is standing firm, doing a very hard thing but one she knows to be right. The artist Dennis Smith, who is one of her descendants, placed this sculpture there on that pier as a tribute to Kristina because her decision that day had eternal significance for generations.

For me this sculpture of Kristina represents each one of you. Like Kristina, you are required to make important and sometimes difficult decisions and choices that will shape not only your future but also the destiny of generations. In these latter days, there are no small decisions. The choices you are making right now are of critical importance. You too may be facing gale-force winds of opposition, adversity, and moral pollution. And yet you are standing immovable and living the gospel in the face of these raging storms in our society. And like Kristina, you can be led by the Holy Ghost. If you live your life in such a way that you can listen to and hear the Holy Ghost, He will help you make correct decisions. In fact, He will tell you "all things what ye should do" (2 Nephi 32:5).

The Holy Ghost is the third member of the Godhead. He is a personage of spirit. He plays a vital role in each of our lives—or He can. It is up to each of us to receive the Holy Ghost as a constant companion after we have been baptized. Personally, I didn't quite understand the import of hands laid on my head when I was eight years old. I have learned to rely constantly on this gift today, but it has taken desire and effort.

In the world in which we live, distractions to the still, small voice of the Spirit come directly into our homes through media, music, and Internet. I once came home from a Church meeting and as soon as I walked into the house, I discerned that something was not right. I called to our son and asked, "Are you watching television?"

To which he replied, "Yes."

Then I said, "Will you turn it off now?"

He did and then came into the entry hall and asked, "How did you know that the show I was watching wasn't consistent with our standards?"

The Holy Ghost must be with us in our homes. He can teach and testify. He can warn and whisper to us. He can prompt and bring peace. He comforts and calms. He can guard and guide us. And He can magnify us in magnificent ways. And He helps us have spiritual gifts, including the gift of discernment.

We have a great work to do. We are "not of the world." We are daughters of God.

We have a great work to do. We are "not of the world" (John 17:14). We are daughters of God. No wonder scripture admonishes us to "arise and shine forth, that [our] light may be a standard for the nations" (D&C 115:5). No wonder the Lord Himself told Emma Smith that she was "an elect lady" (D&C 25:3). No wonder He also told Emma to "walk in the paths of virtue" (D&C 25:2) and to "cleave unto the covenants" (D&C 25:13). His voice to her was His voice to all of His beloved daughters. We are women who have been prepared and reserved to be on the earth now. We are women who have made covenants. Each of us is an elect lady. But the world won't tell us that. The world won't help us understand who we really are and our potential. Only the Spirit will teach us these things, so we must cultivate our ability to receive, respond to, and rely on that Spirit and to screen out those loud and worldly voices.

We live in a world with so many good options and so many good choices. Sometimes all the options are appealing. That is why we need that guidance to know which good choice is right for us individually and for our families. That choice may differ from someone else's choice, but that doesn't mean it is wrong. It means that the Lord is directing our lives individually. What Elder Dallin H. Oaks taught has helped me so much in making decisions about what to do and how to spend my time. He counseled: "We should begin by recognizing the reality that just because something is *good* is not a sufficient reason for doing it. The number of good things we can do far exceeds the time available to accomplish them. Some things are better than good, and these are the things that should command priority attention in our lives" ("Good, Better, Best," *Ensign*, Nov. 2007, 104).

> "Some things are better than good, and these are the things that should command priority attention in our lives."
>
> —ELDER DALLIN H. OAKS

Sister Belle S. Spafford, the ninth Relief Society general president, said: "The average woman today, I believe, would do well to appraise her interests, evaluate the activities in which she is engaged, and then take steps to simplify her life, putting things of first importance first, placing emphasis where the rewards will be greatest and most enduring and ridding herself of the less rewarding activities" (*A Woman's Reach* [1974], 23).

I can think of nothing more deserving of our energy and our time than receiving and recognizing and relying on the Holy Ghost. It is critical that we know how to hear the voice of the Spirit and also that we are able to discern times and places and situations where the Holy Ghost is *not* there. Learning to hear the voice of the Spirit will ensure your success and will tell you all things you should do. It is a precious gift given to all who are members of the Church—the gift to receive the Holy Ghost, a member of the Godhead, to be our constant companion. He is so close to those who are worthy that He is within whispering distance.

Elder David A. Bednar taught that we should "desire, yearn for, and seek the companionship of the Holy Ghost." He taught, "You and I can learn a great lesson about righteous desires from the faithful disciples of the Master described in the Book of Mormon: 'And the twelve did teach the multitude; and behold, they did cause that the multitude should kneel down upon the face of the earth, and should pray unto the Father in the name of Jesus. . . . And they did pray for that which they most desired; and they desired that the Holy Ghost should be given unto them' (3 Nephi 19:6, 9).

Think of the transformation that could occur in the world through the righteous influence of women who know how to receive personal revelation.

"Do we likewise remember to pray earnestly and consistently for that which we should most desire, even the Holy Ghost? Or do we become distracted by the cares of the world and the routine of daily living and take for granted or even neglect this most valuable of all gifts? Receiving the Holy Ghost starts with our sincere and constant desire for His companionship in our lives" ("Receive the Holy Ghost," *Ensign*, Nov. 2010, 95–96).

We must firmly set our hearts on those things that matter most. We cannot allow ourselves to become distracted, distraught, or discouraged. As Nehemiah tried to build a wall around the city of Jerusalem for protection from the enemy, he said, "I am doing a great work, so that I cannot come down" (Nehemiah 6:3). He simply would not be distracted or lured to lower ground. Think of the transformation that could occur in the world through the righteous influence of women who know how to receive personal revelation. What would happen if each of us simply determined not to be lured away from those things that matter most?

What keeps us from hearing the voice of the Spirit? Noise and moral pollution in the form of suggestive music and clothing choices, degrading media, Internet sites, and bad language, to name a few. Perhaps you have noticed that each season's fashions get just a bit more revealing. Each season's TV and movies get just a bit more risqué, and each season's language gets just a bit more abrasive. The adversary does not want you to be focused on what you should do to be successful here on earth. He knows your potential to be a powerful influence for good. He knows your powerful faith and spiritual strength.

There is power in having the companionship of the Holy Ghost! This is a power that the world does not have or understand. As we live in such a way that we are worthy of the guidance and tutoring of a member of the godhead, we can go forward confidently because of the promise that the Holy Ghost will "show unto [us] all things what [we] should do" (2 Nephi 32:5). And what that means is that we are never alone and that it is always possible to know what is right and what is wrong. That is power!

I am struck by a statement Sister Emma Smith made in the first Relief Society meeting. She said, "We are going to do something extraordinary" (Relief Society Minute Book, Nauvoo, Illinois, Mar. 17, 1842, Church History Library, 12).

As I have pondered on how we accomplish the "extraordinary," I have found an answer in the Book of Mormon. Speaking of the sons of Mosiah after their fourteen-year mission, Alma says, "They were still his brethren in the Lord; yea, and they had waxed *strong in the knowledge of the truth;* for they were men *of a sound understanding* and they had searched the scriptures diligently, that they might know the word of God. But this is not all; they had given themselves to much prayer, and fasting; therefore they had the spirit of prophecy, and the spirit of revelation, and when they taught, they taught with power and authority of God" (Alma 17:2–3; emphasis added).

"They had searched the scriptures diligently, that they might know the word of God."

—ALMA 17:2

This is also our formula for becoming "strong in the knowledge of the truth" and "of a sound understanding." We search the scriptures diligently to know the word of God! We pray and fast often to have the spirit of prophecy and revelation and to be able to teach with the power and authority of God.

Elder Bednar added, "Praying, studying, gathering, worshipping, serving, and obeying are not isolated and independent items on a lengthy gospel checklist of things to do. Rather, each of these righteous practices is an important element in an overarching spiritual quest to fulfill the mandate to receive the Holy Ghost. The commandments from God we obey and the inspired counsel from Church leaders we follow principally focus upon obtaining the companionship of the Spirit.

Fundamentally, all gospel teachings and activities are centered on coming unto Christ by receiving the Holy Ghost in our lives" ("Receive the Holy Ghost," *Ensign*, Nov. 2010, 97).

Heavenly Father knows us. We are His precious daughters. He loves us and trusts us with sacred responsibilities, and through the Holy Ghost, He will direct us—even show us—how to fulfill our roles and responsibilities.

6

We Are Disciples of Christ

A few years ago I was released from a calling I loved, Young Women general president. I loved having the opportunity to serve the Lord with all my heart, might, mind, and strength. I loved my associations with the Brethren, with the young women, and with their magnificent mothers and leaders. I loved teaching and training and testifying of the Savior, His virtue, His holy temple, and His role in the great plan of happiness. And when I was released, I wondered for a long time what I could or should do next. Then one day, as I looked at a painting hanging on the wall of our bedroom, of the Savior standing on the shores of the Sea of Galilee, the great question that the Savior asked His Apostles on that shore came into my mind. Peter, "lovest thou me?" (John 21:16). Elaine, lovest thou me?

As you recall, after the Savior's Crucifixion, His Apostles didn't know what to do. Peter's response was, "I go a fishing" (John 21:3). In other words, "I guess I will just go back to my life, my old ways, my previous comfort zone." Several of the other disciples agreed and followed Peter onto a fishing boat to resume the life they had left. That was exactly the plan I was thinking of that morning lying in bed in our home with nowhere to go and nothing to do. *Well,* I reasoned, *I will just go back to my old life—see the kids more, maybe even become a pest. Start playing tennis, run more, have great adventures, go back to book club.* But as I looked at that painting hanging in our bedroom, it spoke to me so personally and I recalled that scene in scripture when the disciples decided to go back to their "old life." They fished all night and never caught a single fish. And then as morning approached and they were headed in, they saw a distant figure standing on the shore and heard him call to them. "Cast the net on the right side of the ship, and ye shall find," he said, and they did so, and caught enough fish that "they were not able to draw it for the multitude of fishes" (John 21:6). John recognized who was speaking and said, "It is the Lord" (John 21:7).

I can only imagine the joy of that reunion, but what happened next is the lesson I learned very personally and want to share. Elder Holland's words in his general conference talk entitled "The First Great Commandment" say it best. He taught:

"After a joyful reunion with the resurrected Jesus, Peter had an exchange with the Savior that I consider the crucial turning point of the apostolic ministry generally and certainly for Peter personally, moving this great rock of a man to a majestic life of devoted service and leadership."

Elder Holland goes on to describe the exchange between Peter and the Lord, when Jesus, having assisted his disciples to catch a huge load of fish, asks his chief Apostle, "Lovest thou me more than these?" Peter's response is immediate: "Yea, Lord; thou knowest that I love thee" (John 21:15). The Lord asks again, and again, and by the third time, "Peter was grieved. . . . And he said unto him, Lord, thou knowest all things; thou knowest that I love thee" (John 21:17).

"To which Jesus responded," Elder Holland continues, ". . . perhaps saying something like: 'Then Peter, why are you here? Why are we back on this same shore, by these same nets, having this same conversation? Wasn't it obvious then and isn't it obvious now that if I want fish, I can get fish? What I need, Peter, are disciples—and I need them forever. I need someone to feed my sheep and save my lambs. I need someone to preach my gospel and defend my faith. I need someone who loves me, truly, truly loves me, and loves what our Father in Heaven has commissioned me to do. Ours is not a feeble message. It is not a fleeting task. It is not hapless; it is not hopeless; it is not to be consigned to the ash heap of history. It is the work of Almighty God, and it is to change the world.'" ("The First Great Commandment," *Ensign*, Nov. 2012, 84).

I believe that once we have experienced the Savior's guidance in our lives, come to know His voice, and learned to be His instrument, we can never be the same again. That day, as I gazed at that painting, I knew I could never go back or depart from the path of discipleship.

As we increase in our discipleship, we will become a greater force for good in the world. Never before has there been a time of such limitless opportunity to connect with others in the world—to serve, to testify, and to make a difference. Having faith in the Savior and purifying our lives enables us to have the constant companionship of the Holy Ghost, and through that power we may accomplish the great things we have been prepared and positioned on this earth to do. "Wherefore, be not weary in well-doing, for ye are laying the foundation of

Never before has there been a time of such limitless opportunity to connect with others in the world—to serve, to testify, and to make a difference.

a great work. And out of small things proceedeth that which is great" (D&C 64:33).

I suppose that many of us, if not all, feel pretty ordinary. But we are not. We should keep in mind that we do not prove our love for the Savior only by doing some great thing. Alma also taught that truly "by small and simple things are great things brought to pass" (Alma 37:6).

There are many ordinary days and events in the scriptures that created extraordinary miracles. I think about an ordinary lad, perhaps sent out by his mother with five loaves and two fishes to sell and bring the money home. Perhaps he was on his way home with those things, having been sent to purchase the family's weekly groceries, or perhaps it was the lunch his mother had sent with him for the day. At any rate, he was willing to give *all* that he had to the disciples of Christ—and an ordinary day became miraculous. An ordinary lad was part of an extraordinary miracle! Not only was he fed, but five thousand others and their spirits were fed the bread of life.

"When Jesus then lifted up his eyes, and saw a great company come unto him, he saith unto Philip, Whence shall we buy bread, that these may eat? And this he said to prove him: for he himself knew what he would do" (John 6:5–6). Philip answered quickly that there was not enough money to buy bread for the multitude. Then Andrew, Peter's brother, said, "There is a lad here, which hath five barley loaves, and two small fishes" (John 6:9). "And when he had taken the five loaves and the two fishes, he looked up to heaven, and blessed, and brake the loaves, and gave them to his disciples to set before them; and the two fishes divided he among them all. And they did all eat, and were filled. And they took up twelve baskets full of the fragments, and of the fishes. And they that did eat of the loaves were about five thousand men" (Mark 6:41–44).

President James E. Faust taught: "It has been said that this church does not necessarily attract great people but more often makes ordinary people great. Many nameless people with gifts equal only to five loaves and two small fishes magnify their callings and serve without attention or recognition, feeding literally thousands" ("Five Loaves and Two Fishes," *Ensign*, May 1994, 5).

Agnes Gonxha Bojaxhiu was one such person, who used her unique gifts and talents to serve the poor and sick of India. She was a nun and said that she was riding a train from Calcutta to the Himalayan foothills when she felt that Christ spoke to her and told her to abandon teaching in order to work in the slums of Calcutta, helping the city's poorest and sickest people. From that time forth, she served the poor and the lepers and established a home where they could be treated and cared for. One by one many people's lives were blessed and changed by this small, quiet woman. She became known as Mother Teresa, although she never gave birth to children of her own. She used her gift of nurturing to bless the lives of millions, but is quoted as saying, "If you can't feed a hundred people, then feed just one." Mother Teresa received the Nobel Peace Prize in 1972, but when she began her work, I don't think she had this recognition in mind at all. Now, having spent a lifetime in unwavering commitment to help those most in need, Mother Teresa is revered as one of the greatest humanitarians of the twentieth century.

One by one many people's lives were blessed and changed by this small, quiet woman. She became known as Mother Teresa, although she never gave birth to children of her own.

You may remember a man named Mister Rogers. He came into our homes with his friendly smile, in his cardigan sweaters made by his mother, and he spent nearly forty years using his beliefs and public television to teach kindness—just kindness—to children. Did it work?

It has been reported that after thieves stole his car, the story was broadcast on television and in newspapers. The car was returned in two days. The note in the car is said to have read: "If we'd known it was yours, we never would have taken it."

Mister Rogers stated his goal simply was to provide "an expression of care every day to each child." In our busy world, I think we often forget that goal. Imagine what would happen if every time you had an opportunity to interact with someone, you used it as an opportunity to provide an expression of care, to make that person feel that his or her needs are important to you and that you care deeply about helping. In doing so, each of us will be developing Christlike attributes that will make us happier and more successful in our professions and in our personal lives.

Each day we are given opportunities to interact with new people and to grow our relationships with people we already know. Mister Rogers knew how important it is to nurture relationships, no matter how small. As a testament of this belief, he personally answered every piece of fan mail he received. He also kept in contact with everyone he ever had on his show. Nobody, young or old, was immune to his simple and genuine caring. Even Koko, the famous gorilla who learned sign language, loved him.

Sometimes we may think that in order to serve others, we have to travel halfway around the world to a remote area and dig a well or build a school. I believe that is not a bad thing to do, but I also feel that expressions of care need to be done one on one—person to person. And they can be done daily, starting in our very own homes.

I recall a morning several months ago when I was extremely busy and feeling especially stressed and pressed for time. I had purchased a white blouse and worn it once and spilled on it. I had thrown it in the washer and had never had the time to iron it. That particular morning, my husband was also very busy with the demands of his business. As I went to the closet to dress, there hanging on the rack was the white blouse! My husband had taken the time to iron it perfectly. That little expression of care went a long way that day and beyond. I am still touched by it.

One of my favorite hymns aptly describes my personal desires and is my polar star. It says, "More fit for the kingdom, more used would I be, more blessed and holy—more, Savior, like thee" ("More Holiness Give Me," *Hymns*, no. 131).

As members of The Church of Jesus Christ of Latter-day Saints, it is our covenant responsibility to serve—to "mourn with those that mourn; yea, and comfort those that stand in need of comfort, and to stand as witnesses of God at all times and in all things, and in all places" (Mosiah 18:9). Having been with you, the noble women all over the world, I have witnessed you do exactly that, and I have been changed.

We need more women who teach kindness and who care deeply about individuals.

In today's society, you are needed. We need more women who teach kindness and who care deeply about individuals. We need more women who concern themselves with the welfare of others before self. We need more women who give their all to the Savior—no matter how small their contribution might seem to them. We need more women who value home and family and serve in that invisible but most formative setting. We need more women like you who are willing to become more holy, more fit for the kingdom, more used, and more like the Savior. We need more women who are willing to use their lives to do what the Savior would do. You are no ordinary women. "Therefore, what manner of men [or women] ought ye to be? Verily I say unto you, even as I am" (3 Nephi 27:27).

I testify that this is the work of the Almighty God, and yes, we are here to change the world! As President Eyring once taught: "[We] are called to represent the Savior. [Our] voice to testify becomes the same as His voice, [our] hands to lift the same as His hands. His work is to bless His Father's spirit children with the opportunity to choose eternal life. So, [our] calling is to bless lives" ("Rise to Your Call," *Ensign*, Nov. 2002, 76).

7

We Are Covenant Women Who Seek Purity and Virtue

In 2010, the top news story of the year was the massive Gulf of Mexico oil spill, triggered by a deadly blast at a rig used by British Petroleum. The April 20th explosion killed eleven workers and unleashed a deep-sea spill that ultimately spewed at least 170 million gallons of crude oil into the gulf. The consequences included a devastating impact to the fishing and tourism industries, a costly cleanup effort, and a $20 billion fund to pay for damages. Government agencies were mobilized, community groups rallied, and individuals went into action to fight the spreading devastation. Many volunteers went to beaches and wetlands and began the painstaking work of cleaning oil off birds and other wildlife. It was an all-out rescue effort, and every individual person's effort made a difference.

Today, right in our homes and communities, there is another equally deadly and devastating pollution spreading into our personal environment. It is moral pollution, and it spews forth constantly at an alarming rate from sources that can come right into our homes. We live in a world that is concerned about cleanliness and purity—the quality of our air and the cleanliness of our environment, the purity of our water, food that is untainted by harmful chemicals and additives, and even the organic nature of our cleaning products. We legislate against pollution and have government-funded protection agencies to ensure that we are not made ill by contaminants that get into our air, our water, or our food supply. Yet society tolerates moral pollution in the form of pornography on billboards, television, the Internet, and in our entertainment and other media. This moral pollution invades our homes and our minds through suggestive lyrics, music, and language. President Boyd K. Packer once said we live in an environment that "is becoming toxic, poisonous to the spirit" ("Faith in the Lord Jesus Christ and His Atonement" [address at seminar for new mission presidents, June 27, 2009], 5).

Jesus taught us to be masters of our bodies and that we should control not only the appetites of the flesh but also the thoughts of our heart (see Matthew 5:27–30). I cannot help but think of what a different society it would be if this were to happen.

Are we doing all we can to clean up our moral environment so that this ecosystem can responsibly support homes and family life? What would happen if the women of the Church unitedly said, "Enough is enough. I will not be a consumer of anything that degrades or objectifies or sexualizes me as a woman, or my daughters, or my granddaughters, or other women, for that matter"?

In this crucial social reform—or "cleanup effort"—one person can make a difference. All over the world, Latter-day Saint women are standing firm and keeping their covenants and declaring their commitment to remain pure and chaste. What would happen if we also spoke out and insisted on moral purity in our society? As covenant women we are uniquely positioned to teach and exemplify virtue and chastity, and I believe we must lead in this effort. If we who have been given so much—including the restored gospel of Jesus Christ—don't lead the world in a return to virtue, who will?

As covenant women we are uniquely positioned to teach and exemplify virtue and chastity, and I believe we must *lead* in this effort.

Now to be clear, the virtue to which I am referring is a pattern of thought and behavior based on high moral standards, and this virtue encompasses sexual purity and chastity. Personal virtue yields strength and is the key that will unlock our power.

I personally find it interesting that Moroni, having seen our day, counsels us to avoid consuming our morality upon our lusts, but instead to seek power and strength in avoiding moral temptation (see Mormon 9:28).

"Alma counseled his son Shiblon to 'bridle all [of his] passions, that [he] may be filled with love' (Alma 38:12). Significantly, disciplining the natural man [or woman] in each of us makes possible a richer, a deeper, and a more enduring love of God and of His children. Love increases through righteous restraint and decreases through impulsive indulgence" (David A. Bednar, "We Believe in Being Chaste," *Ensign*, May 2013, 43–44).

President Marion G. Romney declared: "I can think of no blessings to be more fervently desired than those promised to the pure and the virtuous. Jesus spoke of specific rewards for different virtues but reserved the greatest, so it seems to me, for the pure in heart, 'for they,' said he, 'shall see God' (Matt. 5:8). And not only shall they see the Lord, but they shall feel at home in his presence.

"Here is . . . the Savior's promise: 'Let virtue garnish thy thoughts unceasingly; then shall thy confidence wax strong in the presence of God' (D&C 121:45)" ("Trust in the Lord," *Ensign*, May 1979, 42).

I have spoken about the importance of virtue on many occasions and to many different audiences. Why is virtue, meaning moral purity, so important in today's world? Because, simply stated, it is only through virtue and purity that we can receive the companionship of the Holy Ghost. It can be conferred upon us after baptism, but we must remain pure, because the Holy Ghost does not dwell in unclean temples, "which temple ye are," as Paul taught (1 Corinthians 3:17). Is it possible that in these latter days, when temptations and evil surround us and our families, we sometimes neglect to take advantage of this great gift and power? In the world in which we live, is it possible that we make small compromises, justifying these on the scale of descending mediocrity by rationalizing that "it is not as bad as . . . "? If the world's standards are very low and we're only a little bit higher, we just very well may be heading in the same direction!

"Let virtue garnish thy thoughts unceasingly; then shall thy confidence wax strong in the presence of God."

—D&C 121:45

"We are promised that, as we pursue the pathway of virtue, 'the Holy Ghost shall be [our] constant companion' (D&C 121:46). Thus, living the law of chastity invites some of the greatest blessings men and women can receive in mortality: appropriate spiritual confidence in the presence of family, friends, Church associates, and, ultimately, the Savior" (David A. Bednar, "We Believe in Being Chaste," *Ensign*, May 2013, 44).

We are pure and virtuous women because we are covenant women. As such, we have made sacred covenants to always remember the Savior, to keep His commandments, and to remain chaste, virtuous, and pure. Our identity as covenant women is confirmed in the scriptures: "And behold, ye are the children of the prophets; and ye are of the house of Israel; and ye are of the covenant which the Father made with your fathers, saying unto Abraham: And in thy seed shall all the kindreds of the earth be blessed. The Father having raised me up unto you first, and sent me to bless you in turning away every one of you from his iniquities; and this because ye are the children of the covenant" (3 Nephi 20:25–26).

We are pure and virtuous women because we are covenant women.

We are not ordinary women! Why? Moses said it clearly: "For thou art an holy people unto the Lord thy God: [He] hath chosen thee to be a special people unto himself. . . . The Lord did not set his love upon you, nor choose you, because ye were more in number than any other people; for ye were the fewest of all people: But because the Lord loved you, and because he would keep the oath which he had sworn unto your fathers. . . . Know therefore that the Lord thy God, he is God, the faithful God, which keepeth covenant and mercy with them that love him and keep his commandments to a thousand generations" (Deuteronomy 7:6–9).

What is a covenant? In a gospel sense, a covenant is a binding and solemn compact, agreement, contract, or mutual promise between God and a single person or group of chosen persons. When Alma taught the people at the Waters of Mormon, they were desirous to enter into covenants and become members of the Savior's Church and to become His sons and His daughters. They covenanted to take His name upon them, "to mourn with those that mourn; . . . and to stand as witnesses of God at all times and in all things, and in all places" (Mosiah 18:9). And they were so desirous to do this that they clapped their hands for joy! (see Mosiah 18:11). Later it is recorded that a mighty change of heart occurred and things were never the same again. "Yea, the place of Mormon, the waters of Mormon, the forest of Mormon, how beautiful are they to the eyes of them who there came to the knowledge of their Redeemer" (Mosiah 18:30; see also Mosiah 5:5).

One would think that the first covenants were made by Adam and Eve in the Garden of Eden, but I believe covenants were a part of our premortal experience just as agency was. President Spencer W. Kimball taught: "We made vows, solemn vows, in the heavens before we came to this mortal life. We have made covenants. We made them before we accepted our position here on the earth." He continued, "We committed ourselves to our Heavenly Father, that if He would send us to the earth and give us bodies and give to us the priceless opportunities that earth life afforded, we would keep our lives clean and would marry in the holy temple and would rear a family and teach them righteousness. This was a solemn oath, a solemn promise" ("Be Ye Therefore Perfect" [Salt Lake Institute of Religion devotional, Jan. 10, 1975], 2).

President Kimball further taught, "You and I made a solemn commitment, made an oath that we would do all things whatsoever the Lord our God shall command us" (Spencer W. Kimball, *Church News*, Jan. 18, 1975, 3).

I know of no greater compliment than to have it be said, "She is a covenant keeper."

I know of no greater compliment than to have it be said, "She is a covenant keeper." As women and as mothers, we are uniquely positioned to teach our children the importance of making covenants and then to exemplify for them how to keep those covenants in such a way that they will desire to live worthy to go to the temple.

Virtue, meaning chastity (see D&C 121:45, footnote *b*), is a requirement to enter the temple. It is the golden key that opens temple doors. It is in the temple that we are endowed with power from on high. We also understand that those who are endowed in the temple are "to be taught from on high" (D&C 43:16). When we receive our temple endowment, which means "gift" (see Robert D. Hales, "Blessings of the Temple," *Ensign*, Oct. 2009, 46–49), we are "filled with light" and are able to "[comprehend] all things" (D&C 88:67). Thus, when we receive our endowment in the temple, we also receive the key that unlocks the powers of godliness and the ability to receive knowledge we can obtain in no other way (see D&C 132:18–19).

Nephi said that he "beheld the power of the Lamb of God, that it descended upon the saints of the church of the Lamb, and upon the covenant people of the Lord, . . . and they were armed with righteousness and with the power of God in great glory" (1 Nephi 14:14). In other words, he prophesied about us and that we would prevail in the latter days.

As the Prophet Joseph Smith dedicated the Kirtland Temple, he prayed that we might have the power associated with making and keeping covenants: "We ask thee, Holy Father, that thy servants may go forth from this house armed with thy power, and that thy name may be upon them, and thy glory be round about them, and thine angels have charge over them; . . . That no weapon formed against them shall prosper; . . . And if any people shall rise against this people, that thine anger be kindled against them; And if they shall smite this people thou wilt smite them; thou wilt fight for thy people . . . , that they may be delivered from the hands of all their enemies" (D&C 109:22, 25, 27–28). Thus the Lord gives us an immutable promise (see D&C 93) that everything will work out for our good.

When we attend the temple, the Lord promises each of us that we will come forth from His holy house "endowed with power from on high" (D&C 38:32). We will receive protection and peace from heavenly hosts and "angels [shall have] charge concerning [us]" (Matthew 4:6). This means that we need never face the adversary alone. Keeping our covenants not only gives us moral and spiritual power but also divine power. It means we never have to go through trials, discouragements, or disappointments alone.

Keeping our covenants not only gives us moral and spiritual power but also *divine* power.

The Lord gives a promise assuring each of us, "I will go before your face. I will be on your right hand and on your left, and my Spirit shall be in your hearts, and mine angels round about you, to bear you up" (D&C 84:88). These are the promises to the Lord's covenant people—the house of Israel. I testify that they are true and that they apply here and now and not to some distant future.

A friend of mine was on a humanitarian service trip to

build new classrooms in rural South America. While he was flying in a single-engine plane to a remote Guatemalan village, the engine died. All fourteen passengers aboard the plane knew that a crash-landing on the dense jungle floor below was imminent. For minutes there was silence and an eerie calm as the plane glided and lost altitude. My friend was left to his thoughts about his family and his life. He and the others braced themselves for the inevitable, and in his mind he realized, "I am going to die." His next thought was, "It's okay."

He turned to his coworker, friend, and seatmate, and his friend's last words were, "If it's our time, it's our time."

He nodded in agreement and then thought to himself, "I have kept my covenants." The plane crashed. Eleven of the fourteen did not survive. My friend, badly injured, was pulled from the wreckage by men working in nearby fields just before the plane burst into flames.

His life in the years since has been shaped by this experience. He still suffers effects of the injuries sustained on that day, and yet he moves forward with a renewed power and an enhanced perspective of the grand experience of earth life. This is the kind of confidence we can carry into daily decisions when our choices are accompanied with the most important declaration that can be made—"I have made and kept my covenants."

An integral part of the new and everlasting covenant, which is the restored gospel of Jesus Christ, is the covenant of celestial marriage—the covenant of exaltation. When we are sealed in the temple, we may ultimately become joint heirs to the blessings of the Abrahamic covenant, some of which include an eternal family and the blessings of power and glory and exaltation (see D&C 132:19–20). Through the covenant of celestial marriage we become joint heirs to all the blessings promised to Abraham, Isaac, and Jacob, if we are faithful (see Russell M. Nelson, "Covenants," *Ensign*, Nov. 2011, 86–89).

I will never forget the day my husband, Steve, and I knelt across the altar from each other and looked into each other's eyes. As I knelt in the temple that day, dressed in white, I heard words and made covenants that thrilled me. I felt a powerful connection with the eternities. At the time, I didn't fully comprehend, however, what those covenants meant or would mean in my life, but upon returning to the temple in subsequent years, I grew in my understanding as I witnessed other marriages and sealings. When I entered the temple at different times over the years and saw our valiant sons and our precious daughter, Emi, dressed in white, kneeling at that same altar, making those same covenants, I understood more clearly what covenants really mean in this journey through mortality and was then and am now so grateful for the protection, the power, and the promise associated with making and keeping sacred covenants.

The covenants we make are not restrictive, as some might suppose, but are actually enabling and expanding. They make us free to receive more and more of the blessings that our Father has in store to bestow upon us. Our covenants are like armor. Our Heavenly Father has prepared them for us to protect us and defend us against evil.

Shortly after Nephi separated himself from his brothers and went to a different place, he built a temple. In the verses that follow this account, the scripture states, "We lived after the manner of happiness" (2 Nephi 5:27). I believe that "manner of happiness" was in understanding the plan of happiness, which they learned in the temple, in more clearly understanding the Savior's Atonement, and in making and keeping covenants, which keep us on the path back to God's presence and help us become more like the Savior. Nephi rejoiced in the covenants of the Lord. Thus we rejoice also!

Our covenants are like armor. Our Heavenly Father has prepared them for us to protect us and defend us against evil.

I know there are those whose hearts are broken because covenants have been broken. You may not have a perfect family. Neither do I. But we can continue to strive and try and seek after righteousness. We know that we cannot force others to keep their covenants, but we can keep ours. The power of your covenant and worthy life will pull down blessings on you and on your children, whether they are keeping their covenants or not. Your covenants will help you know what to say and what to do. The Prophet Joseph Smith plainly taught, "When a seal is put upon the father and mother, it secures their posterity so that they cannot be lost, but will be saved by virtue of the covenant of their father and mother" (*History of the Church of Jesus Christ of Latter-day Saints*, 7 vols. [1932–1951], 5:530). And President James E. Faust stated, "Covenants remembered by parents will be remembered by God" ("The Greatest Challenge in the World—Good Parenting," *Ensign*, Nov. 1990, 35).

The power of your covenant and worthy life will pull down blessings on you and on your children.

As Elder M. Russell Ballard so beautifully taught: "Every sister who stands for truth and righteousness diminishes the influence of evil. Every sister who strengthens and protects her family is doing the work of God. Every sister who lives as a woman of God becomes a beacon for others to follow and plants seeds of righteous influence that will be harvested for decades to come. Every sister who makes and keeps sacred covenants becomes an instrument in the hands of God" ("Women of Righteousness," *Ensign*, Apr. 2002, 70).

That is power. That is *our* power.

8

We Are Women of Charity

In Mormon's discourse near the end of the Book of Mormon, he declares that "charity [pure love] never faileth" (Moroni 7:46). The gift of charity comes from the Savior. Charity is there because Christ is there. It endures during the darkest night through difficult trials and on into the sunshine because He does. God so loved us that He gave His Only Begotten Son (see John 3:16). Christ so loved us that His infinite Atonement made it possible for us to return back to our heavenly home and into the presence of God's pure love. Mormon's promise is that such love, the pure love of Christ, is bestowed only upon true followers of Jesus Christ (see Moroni 7:47–48). Christ loved us, and that is how He hoped we would love each other.

I think I will have forever emblazoned in my mind an image

of twin girls that was published in a magazine some years ago. These two little girls were born twelve weeks premature. One of the girls weighed two pounds and was struggling with problems ranging from breathing issues and troubling blood-oxygen levels to heart-rate difficulties. Her sister was two pounds, three ounces, and was considered the stronger of the two.

When the twins were a little less than a month old, the smaller of the two girls went into critical condition. The article recounted, "She began gasping for breath, and her face and stick-thin arms and legs turned bluish-gray. Her heart rate was way up. . . . Her parents watched, terrified that she might die." The nurse did all she could, and nothing seemed to work. She then remembered a common procedure in parts of Europe that helped struggling premature babies, called double-bedding. After the parents gave permission, the nurse put the two babies together in one incubator, hoping it would do some good.

"No sooner had the door of the incubator closed than [the struggling twin] snuggled up to [her sister]—and calmed right down. Within minutes [her] blood-oxygen readings were the best they had been since she was born. And as she dozed, [her sister] wrapped her tiny arm around her smaller sibling" (Nancy Sheehan, "A Sister's Helping Hand," *Reader's Digest,* May 1996, 155–56).

I love this true story because it illustrates so graphically what we can do for others. It is what we, as sisters, can do for each other, what wives can do for husbands and children, and what each of us can do for everyone in the world. We are all God's precious children; each is beloved. We are here to become like Him—to follow the example of His Son and to become as He *is* as we do as He *does.*

Do you ever feel stressed or overwhelmed or have an especially bad day? Perhaps what we all need is an arm around us, a snuggle, or to just feel the warmth and strength of a sister's loving touch.

> "There are no *ordinary* people. You have never talked to a mere mortal."
>
> —C. S. LEWIS

In Doctrine and Covenants 25, the Lord's elect daughters are instructed to "walk in the paths of virtue" (D&C 25:2), to "lay aside the things of this world" (D&C 25:10), and to "cleave unto the covenants which [they have] made" (D&C 25:13). Making and keeping covenants will help us develop spiritual gifts that reflect attributes of the Savior—thus we strive to possess true charity. But each of us must first come to know and understand several things.

FIRST IS OUR IDENTITY—WHO WE ARE AND WHO WE HAVE ALWAYS BEEN. As C. S. Lewis said, "There are no *ordinary* people. You have never talked to a mere mortal" (*The Weight of Glory and Other Addresses* [1965], 15).

The Young Women theme is true doctrine: "We are

daughters of our Heavenly Father, who loves us, and we love Him." His love is infinite and eternal. He loved us so much that He sent His Son to make it possible for us to return to Him once again. When we understand our identity, then that understanding defines all of our actions and interactions. It defines our relationships. Brigham Young taught, "When we look upon the human face we look upon the image of our Father and God; there is a divinity in each person, male and female; there is the heavenly, there is the divine" (*Discourses of Brigham Young,* sel. John A. Widtsoe [1954], 51).

SECOND, WE MUST BE PURE. Moroni's final words to each of us in these latter days—a generation he literally saw—exhorted us to "come unto Christ, and lay hold upon every good gift, and touch not the evil gift, nor the unclean thing" (Moroni 10:30). His exhortation or warning to us was to be pure and virtuous! He was an eyewitness to what happened to a society who had lost their faith, hope, and charity because they had lost their virtue and purity. Why did he exhort us in this manner? Again, it corresponds to his father's message on charity and gaining eternal life and the need to "lay hold upon every good thing . . . until the coming of Christ" (Moroni 7:25). Why? That "when he shall appear we shall be like him, for we shall see him as he is; . . . that we may be purified even as he is pure" (Moroni 7:48).

The principle is never changing—*purity* cannot come from

an *impure* source. Mormon teaches that "a bitter fountain cannot bring forth good water; neither can a good fountain bring forth bitter water" (Moroni 7:11). Thus, pure love cannot come from an impure source. In order to possess pure love, we must *be* pure and virtuous! We are developing patterns of thought and behavior, and they must be based on high moral standards. And our personal purity in thought and action will entitle us to receive the constant companionship of the Holy Ghost.

THIRD, SINCE CHARITY IS A SPIRITUAL GIFT THAT IS BESTOWED UPON US, IT COMES AS A RESULT OF THE RECEPTION OF THE HOLY GHOST. I love the words of President James E. Faust as he taught us about the power we receive from this constant companionship: "I believe the Spirit of the Holy Ghost is the greatest guarantor of inward peace in our unstable world. It can be more mind-expanding and can make us have a better sense of well-being than any chemical or other earthly substance. It will calm nerves; it will breathe peace to our souls. This Comforter can be with us as we seek to improve. It can function as a source of revelation to warn us of impending danger and also help keep us from

> "I believe the Spirit of the Holy Ghost is the greatest guarantor of inward peace in our unstable world."
>
> —PRESIDENT JAMES E. FAUST

making mistakes. It can enhance our natural senses so that we can see more clearly, hear more keenly, and remember what we should remember. It is a way of maximizing *our* happiness" ("The Gift of the Holy Ghost—A Sure Compass," *Ensign*, May 1989, 32–33; emphasis added).

And since the gift of the Holy Ghost is given only to members of the Church, it follows that the fruits and gifts of this Spirit are given in their fullness to Church members. To you and me! Elder Bruce R. McConkie taught this principle: "Men [and women] must receive the gift of the Holy Ghost before that member of the Godhead will take up his abode with them and begin the supernal process of distributing his gifts to them. . . . Thus the gifts of the Spirit are for believing, faithful, righteous people; they are reserved for the saints of God" (*A New Witness for the Articles of Faith* [1985], 370–71).

Bit by bit, week by week, we can develop the ability to love as He would love, until we will become possessed with charity at the last day.

FOURTH, AS WE MAKE AND KEEP OUR COVENANTS, THE PROMISES THOSE COVENANTS CONTAIN WILL HELP US TO BECOME AS THE SAVIOR. Bit by bit, week by week, we can develop the ability to love as He would love, until we will become possessed with charity at the last day. This is a process, not an event. And so we must continually, daily, step by step, keep moving in that direction, always remembering Him and keeping His commandments. We set the tone in our homes; we nurture and love. And charity—the pure love of Christ—never faileth.

We often think of charity as an action. But I think of charity as a state of the heart. It is powerful; it is life changing; it includes the ability to see with new eyes and feel with a new heart. It includes the gift of seeing others as God sees them. The true charity of which I speak makes it possible, and even easy, to look beyond behaviors, outward dress, and appearance to the nobility within. It is a "high-definition" look into an immortal soul. The gift of charity enables the recipient to discern and to know the heart.

Charity is a spiritual gift that is bestowed from the Father to all who are true followers of His Son, Jesus Christ. The gift of charity comes because of the Savior's infinite Atonement. It is more than outward actions—more than casseroles and canned-goods donations—it is a condition of the heart. It is a gift that is earned, sought after, and does not come easily because it is in direct opposition to the natural man. It is *bestowed*, and it doesn't come without patience, practice, repentance, and purity—but it comes. President Ezra Taft Benson described the process this way: "The Lord works from the inside out. The world works from the outside in. The world would take people out of the slums. Christ takes the slums out of people, and then they take themselves out of the slums. The world would mold men by changing their environment. Christ changes men, who then change their environment. The world would shape human behavior, but Christ can change human nature" ("Born of God," *Ensign*, Nov. 1985, 6). Charity can not only transform us; it can transform the world. Imagine what it would be like to live in a society that was constantly striving to possess this heavenly gift. It would be a Zion society! And Zion is the pure in heart—pure hearts, pure people, pure love!

Charity can not only transform us; it can transform the world.

I have been tutored about charity from women all over the world. I have been its recipient. In every country, in every circumstance in which I traveled in my previous calling as the Young Women general president, the women I met exhibited this gift. And as Elder Quentin L. Cook said in the April 2011 general conference, "You are extraordinary!" ("LDS Women Are Incredible!" *Ensign*, May 2011, 18–21). It is a daunting task to go to places where you don't know a soul and to walk into a chapel filled with leaders you have never met and then in a second feel encircled and enveloped by the love in the room—the love of the Savior for them, the love of the Savior in the eyes of those present, the love of the gospel, and the love of others. It is pure, undiluted, unadulterated love—it is charity. You wear the mantle of charity regally!

Shortly after the heartbreaking stillbirth of our daughter's first child at eight and a half months, I had to leave her and return home to Salt Lake City. I was worried about leaving her to face the ensuing gray Chicago winter days with this grief in her heart. Shortly after I returned home, Emi received a package on her doorstep. She opened it to find a statue of a woman, a pioneer woman, standing straight and erect, perhaps looking beyond present difficulties herself. The note accompanying the gift read simply, "You are strong and courageous." This inspired act of pure love from a woman who was prompted by the Spirit has served as a beacon and a light in the days and even years that have followed for my daughter and also for me. That magnificent woman's charity is a beacon in my life to this day. And often on difficult days I find myself saying, "You are strong and courageous."

You are not ordinary. You are the Lord's elect daughters. You can do hard things. You have the constant companionship of the Holy Ghost. You are true followers of Christ. You know what it means to make and keep sacred covenants, and because of that you are striving to "always remember him" in your thoughts and your actions (Moroni 4:3). By your small and simple acts of charity, you are changing the world. Don't get discouraged, and don't give up. Your light and your love make all the difference. Will each of you commit along with me to reach out and light up the life of another daily? It doesn't take much, and it doesn't have to be grand—just a smile, a loving touch, an arm around another, a compliment. Will you do that with me?

The world teaches us that life is all about winning. The Savior teaches us that winners help others succeed. The world teaches that we have no responsibility for another's actions, decisions, or failures. The Savior teaches us that we can change lives and influence choices as we reach out, forget ourselves, and extend a hand of charity. President Thomas S. Monson reminded each of us of this eternal truth when he said: "In a hundred small ways, all of you wear the mantle of charity. Life is perfect for none of us. Rather than being judgmental and critical of each other, may we have the pure love of Christ for our fellow travelers in this journey through life. May we recognize that each one is doing her best to deal with the challenges which come her way, and may we strive to do *our* best to help out" ("Charity Never Faileth," *Ensign*, Nov. 2010, 125).

The world teaches us that life is all about winning. The Savior teaches us that winners help others succeed.

Life teaches us that "charity never faileth" (Moroni 7:46). In fact, we can be assured that "it endureth forever; and whoso is found possessed of it at the last day, it shall be well with him [and her]" (Moroni 7:47).

Like you, I am still a work in progress. But I am grateful to know with an absolute certainty that there is One who, when I trip or stumble or fall, will be there to pick me up, dust me off, encircle me in the arms of His love, and walk with me to the finish line. I testify that He lives and that the more we become like Him in understanding our identity, being pure and virtuous in every aspect of our lives, following the voice of the Spirit, and keeping our covenants, the more our personal charity—our pure love—will never fail.

9

We Can Change the World

I remember a quote I heard a number of years ago from author F. W. Boreham. He was speaking of the events during the Napoleonic Wars in the early part of the nineteenth century: "Men were following, with bated breath, the march of Napoleon, and waiting with feverish impatience for the latest news of the wars. And all the while, in their own homes, babies were being born. But who could think about *babies*? Everybody was thinking about *battles*. . . .

"In one year . . . between Trafalgar and Waterloo, there stole into the world a host of heroes! . . . [in] 1809 . . . Gladstone was born at Liverpool; Alfred Tennyson was born at the Somersby rectory . . . Oliver Wendell Holmes made his first appearance at Massachusetts . . . and Abraham Lincoln drew his first breath at Old Kentucky. Music was enriched by the advent of Frederic Chopin at Warsaw, and of Felix Mendelssohn at Hamburg . . . Elizabeth Barrett Browning [was born] at Durham. . . . But nobody thought of babies. Everybody was thinking of battles. Yet . . . which of the battles of 1809 mattered more than the babies of 1809? . . .

"We fancy that God can only manage His world by big battalions . . . when all the while He is doing it by beautiful babies. . . . When a wrong wants righting, or a work wants doing, or a truth wants preaching, or a continent wants opening, God sends a baby into the world to do it. That is why, long, long ago, a babe was born at Bethlehem" (*Mountains in the Mist: Some Australian Reveries* [1919], 166–67, 169).

It has been observed that "as was the case with the Napoleonic wars, during the years of World War II the news and the eyes of the world were on the battles and not focused on the babies. Yet in 1940, the year many of the western European countries fell and the air over England rained destruction during the Battle of Britain, babies were being born. Three of the babies born that year, you are familiar with. They are Dieter F. Uchtdorf, Quentin L. Cook, and . . . Jeffrey R. Holland. The eyes of the world were not on these babies in 1940—they were following world events—but the Lord's eyes were on them because He knew they would be called upon to help change the world. [These men] came into the world at a very dark time in history: a time many thought would be the end of civilization as we know it; but the Lord has used [them] to help spread the everlasting light of the gospel of Jesus Christ to the world. Each of us has been blessed by [their] ministry" (Paul V. Johnson, "God Sends a Baby" [commencement address given at BYU–Hawaii, Dec. 17, 2011]).

Similarly, that is why Heavenly Father sent us into the world at this pivotal time when opposition is greater than it has ever been, but our opportunity for righteous influence is also greater than it has ever been. It truly is our influence that will shape and change the world. We are part of a plan. *The* plan. Our Heavenly Father has a purpose for your life. He knows exactly where you are. And He will be with you. Though it may seem lonely at times and unpopular, you can go forward with great courage knowing that you are never alone when you are on the Lord's errand. And as you face difficult challenges, you can pray to Him. He will even send His angels to be with you. I testify that this is true! I know that's true because He has done that for me. I know many of you know that is true too because He has done that for you. He will qualify you for every task that is placed before you. He will "lead thee by the hand, and give thee answer to thy prayers" (D&C 112:10). As you exercise your faith

Our Heavenly Father has a purpose for your life. He knows exactly where you are. And He will be with you.

in Jesus Christ, and you pray in His name to our Heavenly Father, He will be with you. He will lead you to a place better than you have any way of comprehending.

I have a saying by Joseph Campbell on my message board at home. It reads: "We must be willing to get rid of the life we've planned, so as to have the life that is waiting for us" (*Reflections on the Art of Living: A Joseph Campbell Companion*, ed. Diane K. Osbon [1991], 18). We can go forward in the strength of the Lord with full confidence in His promises to us. Your life may not unfold exactly as you had planned, but together we can accomplish many seemingly impossible things—and we will change the world.

Your life may not unfold exactly as you had planned, but together we can accomplish many seemingly impossible things—and we will change the world.

Several years ago President Gordon B. Hinckley spoke about the women of the Church—you and me—in a worldwide broadcast. I still remember how I felt as I heard him refer to the women of the Church "as the one bright shining hope in a world that is marching toward [moral] self-destruction" ("Standing Strong and Immovable," *Worldwide Leadership Training Meeting,* Jan. 10, 2004, 20). I still have my dog-eared copy of that speech. It awakened inside of me a sense of who I am and of my eternal identity and possibilities. When imperfect people commit to shining, loving, and serving in our appointed places, as we stretch forth our arms and encircle others, we can know that all the while *we* are also encircled "in the arms of [His] love" (D&C 6:20). I testify that this is true, because I have felt that love from time to time. As women, we must never lose sight of our divine identity and the fact that our influence is powerful and paramount.

What can each of us do now to increase the moral and spiritual influence of women who make and keep sacred covenants? I have made my own personal list of things to work on. You may want to do the same. Your list will be different than mine because we are different and we each have our own divine mission to perform while here on this earth.

Here are some things on my personal list:

- Pray night and morning (and in between)
- Establish a house of order
- Read my scriptures daily
- Repent
- Keep my covenants
- Renew my covenants weekly
- Attend the temple
- Record promptings and impressions
- Follow the prophet with exactness
- Eliminate anything that will detract from the Spirit

- Smile
- Be virtuous in thought and action
- Guard my health
- Love my husband
- Love my children unconditionally
- Spoil my grandchildren
- Don't judge—love!
- Live the Young Women values

And last—dream big! You can do more than you think you can! That is why you are here now at this magnificent time of opportunity. Within your grasp is the opportunity to do something extraordinary!

Dream big!
You can do more than you think you can!

I hope you will believe that you can and are making a difference.

I hope you will have the courage to stand for what you believe, and in that endeavor, inspire others to follow your example.

I hope you will give of your light in every setting and always endeavor to lift the spirits of others, who will then reflect the light to another and another.

Indeed my hope and my prayer for each of you is that somehow in this world you will not be distracted, delayed, discouraged, or disqualified from this, your great mission in life. And that you will press forward to the finish—following our Savior Jesus Christ, who has marked the course and led the way—always aligning your lives with His example. For in this journey you are not alone. He is always there. He will strengthen you. He will enable you. He will lead you by the hand. You have access to great power, and as you learn to access that power you will be able to "act well thy part."

"Hast thou not known? hast thou not heard, that the everlasting God, the Lord, the Creator of the ends of the earth, fainteth not, neither is weary? . . . He giveth power to the faint; and to them that have no might he increaseth strength. . . . But they that wait upon the Lord shall renew their strength; they shall mount up with wings as eagles; they shall run, and not be weary; and they shall walk, and not faint" (Isaiah 40:28–31).

Several years ago, as the LDS Conference Center was being built and nearing completion, I entered that sacred building on the balcony level in a hard hat and safety glasses, ready to vacuum the carpet that my husband was helping to install. Where the rostrum now stands was a front-end loader moving dirt, and the dust in this building was thick. When it settled, it did so on the new carpet. My part was to vacuum. And so I vacuumed and vacuumed and vacuumed. After three days my little vacuum burned up!

The afternoon before the first general conference in that beautiful building, my husband called me. He was about to install the last piece of carpet—under the historic Conference Center pulpit. He asked, "What scripture should I write on the back of this carpet?"

And I said, "Mosiah 18:9: 'Stand as [a witness] of God at all times and in all things, and in all places.'"

In an extremely challenging world, that is what I see women and young women of this Church doing. You are an influence for good. You are virtuous and exemplary, intelligent and industrious. You are making a difference because you *are* different. You are acting well your part.

You are an influence for good. You are virtuous and exemplary, intelligent and industrious. You are making a difference because you are different.

Years ago when I was vacuuming the newly laid carpet in the Conference Center—trying to act well my small part—I didn't realize that I would one day stand with my feet on that very carpet under that magnificent pulpit.

Today as a daughter of God, I stand as a witness that He lives. Jesus is the Christ. He is our Redeemer. It is through His infinite atoning sacrifice that you and I will one day return to live with Him—proven, pure, and sealed in an eternal family. I shall ever praise Him for the privilege of being a woman, a wife, and a mother. I testify that we are led by a prophet of God, and I am grateful for righteous men whose priesthood power blesses my life. And I shall ever be grateful for the strength I receive through the enabling power of the Savior's infinite Atonement as I continue to strive to act well my part.

Remember, "by small and simple things are great things brought to pass" (Alma 37:6).

Here are some ideas of small and simple ways you can become the extraordinary woman the Lord knows and loves.

REFLECT:

- What hard things have you already accomplished in this life? What do those accomplishments tell you about how you can face trials in the future?
- Think of the ways you spend your time every day. Which activities are good, which are better, and which are best? How could you turn some of your "goods" into "betters" or "bests"?
- Why do you think Heavenly Father sent you to earth at exactly this time and in exactly this place? What opportunities do you have to change the world around you, right here and now?

COMMIT:

- As Elder Bednar counseled, "Desire, yearn for, and seek the companionship of the Holy Ghost." Pray for His constant companionship, and keep yourself worthy of this gift.

- Determine that you will keep your mind, your heart, and your home pure, unspotted, and full of virtue.
- Develop patterns of thought and behavior that are based on high moral standards. When an unworthy thought or action creeps in, seek the Lord's help to dismiss and overcome it.

ACT:

- Set a goal to do a hard thing you've never done before. You may want to run a 10K, sign up for an accounting class, learn another language, or make five new friends in your ward. Challenge yourself, and then make a plan and follow through.
- Make, keep, and renew sacred covenants. Attend the temple and partake of the sacrament worthily. Gain the peace of mind that comes from knowing you are living as a woman who has made sacred covenants.
- Change the world as you help others and love others as Christ does. Act on opportunities to show charity every day. Give an expression of care. Dream big. Do something extraordinary!
- Look in the mirror every day and remember you are no ordinary woman!

Index